BASEBALL
THE MATH OF THE GAME

BY THOMAS K. ADAMSON

CAPSTONE PRESS
a capstone imprint

Sports Illustrated KIDS Sports Math is published by Capstone Press,
151 Good Counsel Drive, P.O. Box 669, Mankato, Minnesota 56002.
www.capstonepub.com

Library of Congress Cataloging-in-Publication Data
Adamson, Thomas K., 1970–
  Baseball : the math of the game / by Thomas K. Adamson.
    p. cm.—(Sports Illustrated KIDS. Sports math)
  Includes bibliographical references and index.
  ISBN 978-1-4296-6569-8 (library binding)
  ISBN 978-1-4296-7315-0 (paperback)
  1. Baseball—Juvenile literature. 2. Baseball—Mathematics—Juvenile literature.
  3. Baseball—Statistical methods—Juvenile literature. 4. Arithmetic—Juvenile literature.
  I. Title. II. Series.
  GV867.5.A33 2012
  796.357—dc22   2011004483

Editorial Credits
Anthony Wacholtz, editor; Alison Thiele, designer; Eric Gohl, media researcher;
  Eric Manske, production specialist

Photo Credits
Library of Congress, 14 (top), 34
Newscom/Icon SMI 132/Dustin Bradford, 14 (bottom)
Shutterstock/Debra Hughes, design element; Petr Vaclavek, design element; Rocket400
  Studio, 8, 45 (front)
Sports Illustrated/Al Tielemans, cover (front), 4–5, 16 (bottom), 20, 22 (bottom), 26
  (top), 32, 33 (all), 36; Chuck Solomon, 12, 28 (bottom), 30–31; DamianStrohmeyer,
  11 (top), 13 (left), 15, 25, 28 (top), 38, 39, 42–43, 44–45; David E. Klutho, 6,
  24, 29 (bottom); John Biever, cover (back), 10, 16 (top), 17, 18, 19, 26 (bottom),
  27, 41 (bottom); John G. Zimmerman, 13 (right), 37; John W. McDonough, 9, 35;
  Lane Stewart, 11 (bottom); Robert Beck, 1, 21, 22–23, 23 (bottom), 29 (top), 31
  (front), 40, 41 (top); Simon Bruty, 7

Printed in the United States of America in Melrose Park, Illinois.
032011   006112LKF11

TABLE OF CONTENTS

□ MATH AND BASEBALL

Baseball is a great sport for fans who love statistics. When you watch a game on TV or listen to it on the radio, the announcers provide a steady stream of numbers and stats. They can discuss a batter's average, home runs, and runs batted in. The announcers can talk about the batter's average against the pitcher, his average with runners in scoring position, his average against a left-handed pitcher, and so on. The stats on the back of a baseball card tell you a lot about a player, but there is even more we can do with those numbers.

Baseball might have more stats than any other sport. There is plenty of data to work with, and Major League Baseball has kept track of many stats for a long time. You can find hitting stats that go back to the late 1800s. These stats have given fans plenty to discuss and argue about for well over a century.

Stats are math, and they give us a way to compare players. But baseball is more than just stats. There is plenty of math to be found around the field. Geometry and physics help us better understand how the game is played. So grab your calculator, and let's head to the ballpark!

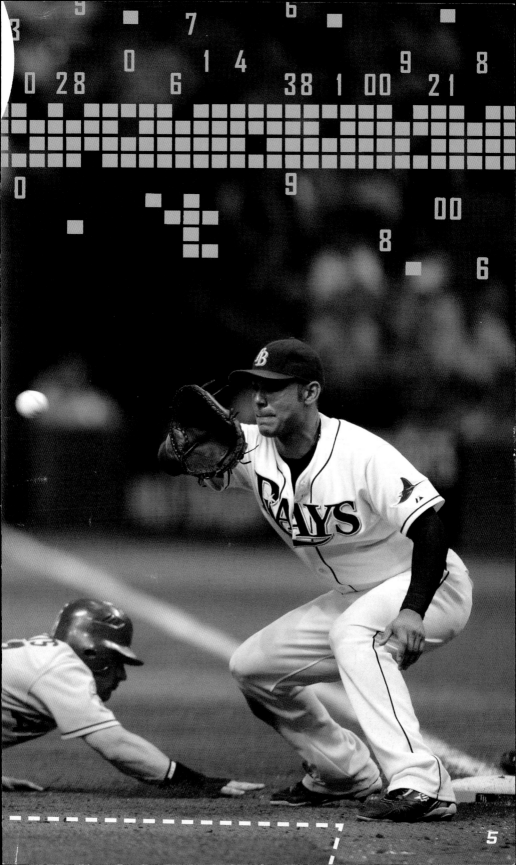

CHAPTER 1

Get out your ruler—the ballpark is a great place to do some measuring. Measurements in professional baseball are precise. The distance from home plate to first base is exactly 90 feet. In fact, it's 90 feet between every base. Knowing that, we can calculate the area of the infield.

area = width * height

The infield is a square, so the area of the infield equals 90 feet times 90 feet, or 8,100 square feet. Luckily, a base runner only has to run between bases. To find out how far it is around all the bases, we can calculate the perimeter of the square.

90 feet + 90 + 90 + 90 = 360 feet

90 ft

90 ft

90 ft

90 ft

One mile is 5,280 feet, so the distance a base runner has to run around the bases and back to home is only about 0.07 miles.

$$\frac{360 \text{ feet}}{5,280 \text{ feet/mile}} = \frac{0.0681818, \text{ or}}{0.07 \text{ miles}}$$

Seven-hundredths of a mile is the distance a runner covers if he runs straight to each base. More often runners round the bases so they don't have to slow down. That means they run more than 0.07 miles, but they do so more quickly.

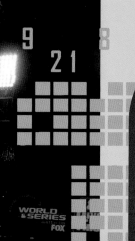

AREA OF THE PITCHER'S MOUND

The pitcher's mound is a circle, so finding its area is a little more complicated. The formula for finding the area of a circle is

$$area = pi * r^2$$

All you need to know to figure out the area of a circle is the radius or the diameter. The radius is the length of a line drawn from the center of a circle to its edge. The diameter is the length of a line drawn through the center of a circle.

9 Feet

The diameter of the pitcher's mound is 18 feet. Because the radius is half the length of the diameter, we can use 9 feet in the equation. Pi is always 3.14159, or 3.14.

$$area = 3.14 * 9^2 = 254.34$$

The area of the pitcher's mound is about 254 square feet. Although it's a circle, "square" is always used in the measurement for area.

Now you know the distance around the bases, but how about the whole field? All ballparks are different. However, the official MLB rules say that the distance from home plate to the outfield wall along the foul lines should be at least 320 feet and at least 400 feet to the center field wall.

STANDINGS

When we get near the end of the regular baseball season, we start hearing a lot about magic numbers. This number tells us what a team needs to clinch a playoff spot. A team's magic number is a combination of 1) the number of wins a team needs and 2) the number of losses by the team's closest opponent in the division. Let's look at a sample division.

NL WEST	W	L	GB
SAN DIEGO PADRES	85	65	--
LOS ANGELES DODGERS	83	67	2
SAN FRANCISCO GIANTS	80	69	4.5
COLORADO ROCKIES	71	79	14
ARIZONA DIAMONDBACKS	60	89	24.5

The Dodgers have two fewer wins and two more losses than the division-leading Padres. That makes them two games behind (GB) San Diego in the division. If Los Angeles won their next two games and San Diego lost their next two games, they would be tied for the division lead.

In 2001 the Seattle Mariners tied a MLB record for wins in a season when they won 116 games. In 1906 the Chicago Cubs also won 116 games. But in 1906 the regular season was 155 games instead of 162. So the Cubs' win percentage was higher.

$$116 / 162 = .716 \qquad 116 / 155 = .748$$

What does San Diego need to do to clinch the division? With 12 games left to play, there are a few ways that San Diego can clinch. If the Padres win at least 11 games, they automatically win the division. Even if Los Angeles won the rest of its games, they would still end up one game behind San Diego. Therefore, San Diego's magic number is 11. However, San Diego would not have to win that many games if Los Angeles loses some. Every win by the Padres or loss by the Dodgers lowers San Diego's magic number. Once that magic number gets down to zero, San Diego's going to the playoffs.

ONE GAME AT A TIME

Teams usually aren't thinking about the playoffs until late in the season. That's why it's helpful for a team to focus on winning each series. Although there are some four-game series, most series are three games. If a team wins all of its series, that would be at least two out of three wins, or a .667 win percentage. Take that percentage (.667) times the number of games in a season (162), and that puts the team on pace for 108 wins—a great season! That's why fans emphasize the importance of winning series throughout the season.

Batting average (AVG) is one of the most well-known stats in baseball. Batting average is calculated by dividing a batter's hits by his at bats.

$$AVG = hits / at\ bats$$

For example, in 2010 Texas Rangers outfielder Josh Hamilton had 186 hits in 518 at bats.

$$Hamilton's\ AVG = 186 / 518 = .3590733$$

Rounded to three decimal places, Hamilton's average was .359. That was good enough to be the best in Major League Baseball that year. To show how significant batting average is seen by players, fans, and baseball experts, Hamilton not only won the batting title that season, he was also named the AL Most Valuable Player.

JOSH HAMILTON

In figuring a player's batting average, it's important to know what counts and what doesn't count as an at bat. If a batter walks (BB), that plate appearance does not count as an at bat. A hitter who gets four plate appearances in a game and strikes out once and walks three times gets a batting average of .000, even though he made it on base 75 percent of the time. Other plate appearances that don't count as at bats are sacrifice flies (SF), sacrifice bunts, or being hit by a pitch (HBP).

A player isn't charged with a plate appearance if he's hit by a pitch. That means the HBP doesn't affect his batting average.

TRIPLE CROWN

Batting average is one of the three Triple Crown stats. The others are runs batted in and home runs. The Triple Crown award goes to a batter who leads his league (AL or NL) in all three categories. It doesn't happen very often. The last time was in 1967, when Carl Yastrzemski batted .326 and hit 44 home runs and 121 RBIs.

CARL YASTRZEMSKI

Some people don't think that a player's average is a good measure of his hitting skills. Batting average does not take into account extra base hits. With batting average, a triple is just as good as a single, even though the batter gets three bases instead of just one.

Also, in a real game situation, a two-out single in the ninth inning of a tie game with a runner on second is much more valuable than a two-out single in the ninth inning with no one on and a six-run lead. Especially when the next batter strikes out. But batting average counts them the same.

While On Base Percentage (OBP) isn't the perfect measure of a player's hitting skills, it has more depth because it shows how often a batter reaches base. It figures in not just hits but also walks, hit by pitch, and sacrifice flies. Baseball doesn't have a clock—it has outs. It's important to know how often a batter avoids outs, and that's what OBP tells us. The OBP formula is:

$$OBP = \frac{H + BB + HBP}{AB + BB + HBP + SF}$$

Here are three players' hitting stats from 2010:

	JASON HEYWARD	MATT HOLLIDAY	JOE MAUER
AB	520	596	510
H	144	186	167
BB	91	69	65
HBP	10	8	3
SF	2	2	6

Who had the best OBP among Heyward, Holliday, and Mauer?

ANSWER: Joe Mauer
(Mauer .402; Heyward .393; Holliday .390)

Ted Williams has the best career OBP in MLB history at .482.

TED WILLIAMS

SLUGGING PERCENTAGE

Slugging percentage (SLG%) describes a batter's ability to get extra base hits, whether it's from running out a triple or belting a home run. SLG% does not count walks—this stat is about power and getting as many bases as possible. The SLG% formula is

SLG% = total bases / at bats

To calculate a player's total bases, you need to know how many singles, doubles, triples, and home runs were hit. Then multiply the doubles by 2, the triples by 3, and the home runs by 4. The last step is to add all four numbers together.

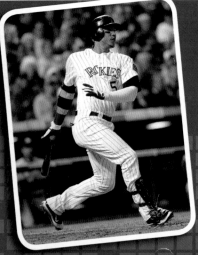

BABE RUTH

Here are Babe Ruth's hitting stats for 1920, his first year with the Yankees:

AB	458
SINGLES	73
DOUBLES	36
TRIPLES	9
HR	54

His SLG% that season was .847.

$$\frac{73 + (36 * 2) + (9 * 3) + (54 * 4)}{458} = .847$$

Ruth's SLG% was the best in history until 2001. That year Barry Bonds broke the record with a .863 SLG%.

Which player had the higher SLG% in 2010?

	ALBERT PUJOLS	CARLOS GONZALEZ
AB	587	587
SINGLES	101	120
DOUBLES	39	34
TRIPLES	1	9
HR	42	34

ANSWER: Carlos Gonzalez (Gonzalez: .598; Pujols .596)

14

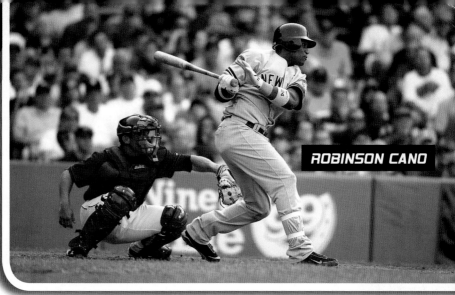

ROBINSON CANO

BASEBALL PIE

To help analyze a hitter's stats, we can make a pie graph. See Robinson Cano's plate appearances (PA) from 2010 in the chart (right).

What percentage of Cano's plate appearances were home runs?
To calculate this percentage, divide the number of HRs by the number of PA.

$$\frac{29 \ HR}{696 \ PA} = .042, \ or \ 4.2\%$$

In 2010 Cano hit a HR 4.2 percent of the time, or about once every 24 plate appearances. What about his ability to hit singles?

PA	696
1B	127
2B	41
3B	3
HR	29
BB	57
HBP	8
SF	5
OUTS OR REACHED BY ERROR	426

$$\frac{127 \ singles}{696 \ PA} = 18.2\%$$

Cano got a single once every 5.5 plate appearances— not bad at all!

MULTIPLE HIT GAMES

Baseball is a game of stats. It's fun and easy to compare players' batting averages, home runs, and on base percentages. But instead of looking at these straight averages, sometimes it's helpful to look at how many multiple hit games a player has. A batter who has a .250 AVG will average one hit for every four at bats, but the distribution of his hits will vary throughout the season.

SPLITS

Sometimes players' stats are split into categories. A few common splits are how well a batter does against left-handed pitchers vs. right-handed pitchers, on turf or grass, and during the day or night.

Michael Young of the Texas Rangers is well-known for pounding out two or more hits per game. Over 10 seasons he has compiled 543 multihit games. See how many hits he had per game based on the number of at bats in the chart for the 2010 season.

There are a couple of ways to use the data in the chart. You can compare the totals to the number of games played (255) to see what percentage of his at bats were multihit games. He had 41 two-hit games, 12 three-hit games, and two four-hit games. Add the three totals (41 + 12 + 2 = 55) and divide it by the number of games (55 / 255). That means Young had a multihit game 21.6 percent of the time in 2010.

AT BATS	HITS				
	0	1	2	3	4
6	1	2	2	X	X
5	8	16	16	4	1
4	24	31	20	8	1
3	7	9	3	X	X
2	2	2	X	X	X
TOTALS	42	60	41	12	2

Based on this table, how many times did Young go 3-5 in 2010?

ANSWER: 4

SWING TIMING

When a 90-mph fastball is coming your way, you barely have time to blink before it zooms past you. But how much time do you actually have to swing your bat?

It's 60 feet 6 inches from the pitcher's mound to home plate. So if the pitcher throws a 90-mph fastball, we can figure out how long it takes for the ball to cross home plate. First we have to convert miles to feet. There are 5,280 feet in a mile, so a 90-mph fastball goes 475,200 feet per hour.

What is that in feet per second? There are 60 seconds in a minute, and 60 minutes in an hour. So if we divide 475,200 by 60 twice, we get 132 feet per second. The pitcher is only 60 feet 6 inches away, so it takes 0.46 seconds (60.5 / 132) for the ball to arrive at home plate. Because the pitcher's release point is less than 60.5 feet away, it's actually less time than that. So the batter better be ready!

FOUL BALL

Foul balls are common because the ball and barrel of the bat are round. If the ball makes contact with the bat in the middle of the barrel's width, the ball goes straight. But it's pretty hard to do that. The ball often makes contact with the barrel a bit high or low, making the baseball spin off to one side or go straight up.

The batter has more time to swing if a 75-mph changeup is heading his way. With the same calculations, a 75-mph changeup goes 396,000 feet per hour, or 110 feet per second. The changeup takes 0.55 seconds to cross home plate. That's 0.09 seconds slower than the 90-mph fastball.

Although it doesn't seem like a lot of time, 0.09 seconds may be just enough for the batter to make contact. The 0.09 seconds may also be enough difference to throw off a batter's timing if he expects a fastball.

Now consider this from the pitcher's point of view. After his follow-through, he's about 55 feet from the batter. He has to change from a pitcher to a fielder very quickly, and the ball may come back at him even faster than his 90-mph fastball.

"During my 18 years I came to bat almost 10,000 times. I struck out about 1,700 times and walked maybe 1,800 times. You figure a ball player will average about 500 at bats a season. That means I played seven years in the major leagues without even hitting the ball."—Mickey Mantle

One of the most popular stats for pitchers is earned run average. ERA tells us, on average, how many earned runs a pitcher allows over nine innings. ERA is calculated by taking the total number of earned runs divided by the number of innings pitched. Then the result is multiplied by 9.

$$ERA = (ER / IP) * 9$$

JON LESTER

For example, Jon Lester allowed 75 earned runs in 208 innings in 2010.

$$ERA = (75 / 208) * 9$$
$$ERA = .3606 * 9$$
$$ERA = 3.25$$

Bob Gibson of the St. Louis Cardinals had the best single-season ERA of the modern era in 1968. He started 34 games and had a win-loss record of 22–9. In 304⅔ IP he allowed only 38 earned runs. That comes to an amazing 1.12 ERA for the season.

Sometimes the total IP for a pitcher is shown with a .1 or a .2 after the number. But how can you throw one-tenth of an inning?

Those numbers represent one-third (.333) and two-thirds (.667) of an inning. Each out is one-third of an inning. So a starting pitcher is credited for 5 ⅓ IP if he leaves the game with one out in the sixth inning. You would calculate the ERA the same way.

In 2010 Felix Hernandez gave up 63 earned runs in 249.2 innings.

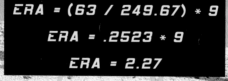

$$ERA = (63 / 249.67) * 9$$
$$ERA = .2523 * 9$$
$$ERA = 2.27$$

EARNED VS. UNEARNED

What's the difference between an earned run and an unearned run? An earned run is a run that the pitcher is responsible for. If a run was scored from a walk and a double, for example, the pitcher would receive an earned run. If a run scores because of a fielder's error, it's an unearned run because it wasn't the pitcher's fault.

WHIP

To go with ERA, WHIP is a popular pitching stat that includes walks and hits.

$$WHIP = (Walk + Hits) / IP$$

WHIP shows an average of how many base runners a pitcher allows per inning. This stat is especially helpful to gauge the value of relief pitchers, since win-loss percentage doesn't tell you much about them. WHIP doesn't include how many runs a pitcher allows per inning. But because a run can't score without base runners, a pitcher's WHIP is a good measure of his ability to get people out.

RAFAEL SORIANO

Let's see how this works for a couple of relievers from the 2010 season. Former Rays closer Rafael Soriano pitched 62.1 innings, allowing 36 hits and 14 walks.

$$WHIP = (36 + 14) / 62.1$$
$$WHIP = 50 / 62.1 = 0.81$$

BRIAN WILSON

Giants closer Brian Wilson had a similar ERA (1.81) as Soriano (1.73), but Wilson's WHIP was 1.20. He gave up 26 more hits and 12 more walks than Soriano. Usually when a pitcher has a low ERA and a high WHIP, he is good at stranding runners on the bases.

WIN-LOSS

Win-Loss (W-L) record is another common stat for pitching. A pitcher gets credit for a win if his team is leading when he leaves the game and they go on to win. But a starter must complete five innings to get credit for the win, and his team must always have the lead after he leaves the game.

Win percentage is a quick calculation.

$$\text{win percentage} = \text{wins} / (\text{wins} + \text{losses})$$

Adam Wainwright's W-L record in 2010 was 20–11. What was his win percentage?

$$\text{win percentage} = 20 / (20 + 11)$$
$$20 / 31 = .6451612$$

Win percentage is rounded to three decimals (.645). This can also be said as 64.5%.

ADAM WAINWRIGHT

QUALITY START

A quality start is awarded to a starting pitcher who completes at least six innings while allowing three earned runs or fewer.

A pitcher's win-loss record only tells part of the story. To determine a pitcher's ability, you need to look at his ERA, WHIP, and other stats too.

In 2010 Felix Hernandez of the Seattle Mariners led the league with a 2.27 ERA, and his WHIP was 1.06—a very good number. However, his win-loss record was 13–12. If you only look at his win-loss record, you wouldn't know that Hernandez had a great year.

PHIL HUGHES

On the other hand, Phil Hughes of the New York Yankees had an 18–8 record, but he had a 4.19 ERA and a 1.25 WHIP. Although his ERA and WHIP weren't as good as Hernandez's, the Yankees' offense helped him win more games.

The best single-season W-L percentage was in 1959, when Roy Face of the Pittsburgh Pirates had an 18–1 record (94.7 percent).

K/IP

Strikeouts per inning (K/IP) is another pitching stat that is used to determine a pitcher's worth. In 2010 Roy Halladay threw 208 strikeouts in 239 innings. Halladay's K/IP was 208 Ks / 239 innings = 0.87. Multiply the result by 9 to get an average of how many strikeouts he would throw over nine innings. Halladay's K/9 IP was 7.8.

ROY HALLADAY

TIM LINCECUM

Tim Lincecum of the San Francisco Giants led the majors with a K/9 IP ratio of 9.79. Lincecum's K/9 IP ratio has been so good that he has led the majors the last three years and reached a 10.51 ratio in 2009.

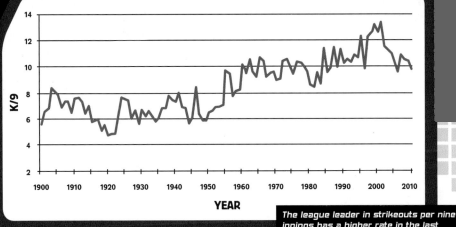

K/9 LEADERS IN MLB HISTORY

K/9

YEAR

The league leader in strikeouts per nine innings has a higher rate in the last few decades than in the early 1900s.

WHEN DOES 4 = 3?

How can a pitcher get four strikeouts in one inning? The math seems impossible, but it has happened 55 times through 2010. Chuck Finley did it three times!

If the catcher can't hold on to strike three, the batter can try to reach first base. Even if the batter makes it to first, the pitcher still gets credit for the K, but it's not recorded as an out. If the pitcher strikes out the other three batters, he will get four Ks in one inning.

Manny Parra threw four strikeouts in an inning on June 6, 2010.

FIELDING STATS

The stats don't end with hitting and pitching. Baseball even has stats for fielding. One common stat is fielding percentage. This stat shows how well players are doing in the field. The only thing that can lower a fielder's fielding percentage is an error.

$$\text{fielding percentage} = \frac{(putouts + assists)}{(putouts + assists + errors)}$$

DUSTIN PEDROIA

GROUNDBALLS

Fielders charge groundballs to get to the baseball quicker. An average runner will reach first base in 4.2 seconds. Charging the grounder gives the fielder a little extra time to throw the runner out.

HANLEY RAMIREZ

In 2010 David Wright had 110 putouts and 321 assists, and he committed 20 errors.

$$(110 + 321) / (110 + 321 + 20)$$

$$431 / 451 = .956$$

Nobody's perfect, but Albert Pujols of the St. Louis Cardinals came close with a .998 fielding percentage in 2010. That's especially impressive considering he had 1,458 putouts and 157 assists with only four errors.

ALBERT PUJOLS

There's a lot happening when a runner tries to steal a base. Knowing that it's 90 feet between the bases, we can figure out how far it is from home plate to second base. Then we can find out how much time a catcher has to throw out a base runner trying to steal second base.

The infield of a baseball field forms a square. If you draw a line from home to second base, the square becomes two right triangles. Using a formula called the Pythagorean theorem, we can calculate the distance from the catcher to second base.

Pythagorean theorem: $a^2 + b^2 = c^2$

The Pythagorean theorem is used to find the line lengths of a right triangle. If you have two of the lengths, the theorem allows you to find the third. In the equation a and b are the two shorter sides of the triangle, and c is the hypotenuse. On the baseball field, the line from home to second is the hypotenuse of the right triangle.

$$90^2 + 90^2 = c^2$$

$$8100 + 8100 = c^2$$

$$c^2 = 16,200$$

Now take the square root of 16,200 to get the answer. The distance from the catcher to second base is 127.28 feet.

How much time does a base runner on first base have to steal second? First we need to figure out how far he has to run. It's 90 feet between the bases, but base runners almost always lead off. So he really only has to go about 80 feet.

The rest depends on how fast the catcher can get the ball to second base. If he throws 75 mph it would take the ball about 1.1 seconds to get to second base. Add the time it took for the pitcher to throw the pitch (.46 seconds for a fastball), and it comes to 1.56 seconds. That's about how much time the runner has to steal second. Even if you add about half a second for the catcher to catch the pitch, pull the ball out of his mitt, step, and throw, that's not much time for the base runner to cover 80 feet.

c

90 ft b

90 ft

a

CHAPTER 4

RATIOS

A good way to determine players' skills is to compare stats for a single player. Sometimes you'll find that even though a player excels in one category, he might hurt his team in another category. For example, in 2010 Mark Reynolds hit 32 HRs with 79 runs and 85 RBIs. Not bad for any player, but he only had a .198 batting average.

One way to determine a player's abilities at the plate is to look at his strikeout-to-walk ratio (K/BB). Although Reynolds hit a lot of home runs and drove in runs, he struck out 211 times compared to only 83 walks.

The strikeout-to-walk ratio is just as important for pitchers. Even if a pitcher has a high strikeout rate, he may not be a great pitcher if he walks a lot of batters. That's why it's important to compare a pitcher's strikeouts and walks.

MARK REYNOLDS

Over 212.1 innings pitched in 2010, Cliff Lee struck out 185 batters and walked only 18. His K/BB ratio was 185 / 18 = 10.28—the best in the majors.

Now compare that to Tim Lincecum's. His K/BB ratio was 231/76, or 3.04. So although Lincecum struck out 46 more batters than Lee, he also walked four times as many players.

CLIFF LEE

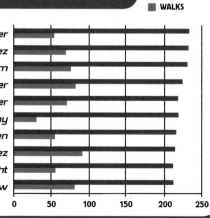

K / BB RATIO IN 2010

■ STRIKEOUTS
■ WALKS

	0	50	100	150	200	250
Jered Weaver						
Felix Hernandez						
Tim Lincecum						
Jon Lester						
Justin Verlander						
Roy Halladay						
Dan Haren						
Ubaldo Jimenez						
Adam Wainwright						
Clayton Kershaw						

TIM LINCECUM

TRENDS

We can use numbers and statistics to discover trends throughout baseball history. The game of baseball hasn't always been played the same way. Look at the graph of the number of complete games pitchers have played.

COMPLETE GAMES LEADERS

It's been awhile since a pitcher has reached 10 complete games in one season. From the downward trend shown on the chart, we're not likely to see that feat accomplished again soon.

Starting pitchers used to rack up a lot more wins than they do now. Today only a few starting pitchers reach 35 games each season. A hundred years ago, starters pitched more than 40 games per season, and they completed many of them. For example, in 1899 Cy Young started 42 games and completed 40 of them. He worked 369.1 innings. The last time someone pitched more than 300 innings in one season was in 1980 when Steve Carlton worked 304 innings for the Phillies.

CY YOUNG

Another trend that has changed since the early 1900s is the use of closers. Back then managers used several pitchers to close out games. Over time more managers decided to pick one "go to" relief pitcher to close all the games.

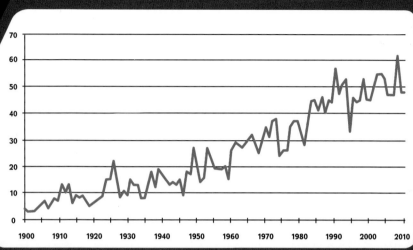

MAJOR LEAGUE SAVES LEADERS

Over 100 years, you can see an upward trend in the major league saves leader. But will the trend continue? Not likely. Closers can't pitch every day, and teams can't win every game. That's why the trend has evened out in the last few decades. Francisco Rodriguez's record 62 saves with the Angels in 2008 will be tough to beat.

When looking at trends, you may notice places where the data changes abruptly. For example, if you look at the saves leaders graph, you'll notice a drop in 1994. While it could be a coincidence, it's important to see if there is a reason behind the temporary drop. In 1994 there was a strike that ended the season with 47 games left to play. That's why the saves leader that year was lower than in the other years that decade.

FRANCISCO RODRIGUEZ

PREDICTIONS

We can use math to make predictions about what is likely to happen to players throughout the course of a season. For example, if a pitcher throws 50 Ks over his first nine starts of the season, we can calculate how many Ks he will end the season with if he keeps up the same pace. All you need is a few of the player's stats, and cross multiplication will take care of the rest.

In 2000 Randy Johnson pitched in 35 games. By the end of April, he had already racked up 64 Ks in six games. With just those few stats, fans could predict how many strikeouts Johnson would end the season with. The problem can be stated like this: 64 is to 6, as x is to 35.

$$\frac{64}{6} = \frac{x}{35}$$

Using cross multiplication, we can solve for x, a variable that stands for the number of strikeouts expected over 35 games.

$$64 * 35 = 6 * x$$
$$2,240 = 6x$$

To solve for x, divide each side by 6. That will leave x by itself.

$$2,240 / 6 = 6x / 6$$
$$2,240 / 6 = x$$
$$x = 373.33$$

RANDY JOHNSON

So by the end of April, Johnson was on a pace to throw 373 Ks over the entire season. Sound incredible? Not for the Big Unit. He tallied 347 Ks that season. Although the 373 K prediction wasn't exact, it wasn't off by much.

These predictions get more accurate as the season progresses. To illustrate the point, let's look at the great 1961 home run chase. Roger Maris of the New York Yankees electrified baseball fans as he chased Babe Ruth's single-season HR record of 60. At the halfway point in the season (81 games), Maris had hit 32 home runs.

$$\frac{32}{81} = \frac{x}{162}$$

$$32 * 162 = 81 * x$$
$$5,184 = 81x$$

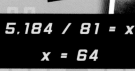

$$5,184 / 81 = x$$
$$x = 64$$

ROGER MARIS

MARIS OF THE YANKEES

Sports Illustrat

OCTOBER 2, 1961 25 CENTS

WOR SER PREV

That's why people were so excited. At this point Maris was on pace to hit 64 HRs, well ahead of the Babe's record. In the fourth inning of the final game of the regular season, Maris clobbered his 61st home run over the wall at Yankee Stadium. Although off by three home runs, the prediction that Maris would break the record was correct.

CORRELATIONS

Over the course of an entire season, does the team that scored the most overall runs end up with the best win percentage? It makes sense that the more runs a team scores, the more wins it will have. We can use a scatter plot to see if there is any relation, called a correlation, between runs scored and win percentage.

The runs scored and wins for the 2010 season are plotted on the graph below. The points on the graph gather along the diagonal line that goes from the lower left to the upper right. That means the data have a positive correlation. It shows that if a team scores a lot of runs over the course of a season, it will probably have more wins.

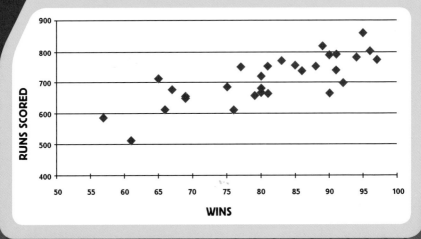

2010 MLB TEAMS (WINS VS. RUNS SCORED)

Now let's see if there is a correlation between stats for individual players. For one example, is there a correlation between the number of a pitcher's strikeouts and walks? If a pitcher throws a lot of strikeouts, does that mean he'll give up a lot of walks too?

A scatter plot for the top 100 strikeout pitchers in 2010 looks different from the first scatter plot. The points are scattered throughout the graph. That means there is no correlation between a pitcher's strikeouts and walks. Cliff Lee threw 185 strikeouts and only 18 walks in 2010. His impressively low number of walks did not affect his strikeout ability.

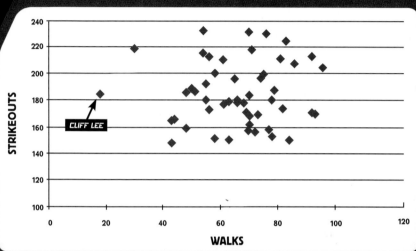

2010 MLB PITCHERS (STRIKEOUTS VS. WALKS)

Try to make scatter plots for other stats to see if they correlate. Try home runs and RBIs. If a batter hits a lot of home runs, does that mean he also has a lot of RBIs? Similarly, can a player rack up a high number of RBIs if he doesn't hit many home runs?

CLIFF LEE

ALL IN A DAY'S WORK

Stats are always changing. Each game that goes by can affect a player's stats. If a batter goes 0-4 in a game, his average will certainly go down. But by how much depends on how much of the season has been played.

By April 10, 2010, Miguel Cabrera had already recorded nine hits in 23 at bats. His batting average after five games was a remarkable .450. On April 11 Cabrera went 3-3, which raised his average a whopping 72 points to .522. Over the next three games, though, he went 2-11, dropping his average 110 points to .412. Because it was so early in the season, every at bat made his average jump or plummet.

MIGUEL CABRERA

The more at bats a player has, the less his stats are affected by the at bat. On July 6 Cabrera was batting .339. That day he went 3-5, but it only raised his average to .343. On September 17, with less than a week to go in the regular season, he was hitting .332. After two 0-5 games, his average only dropped to .326. By that point in the season, he had already had more than 500 at bats, so two hitless games had little effect on his average.

Stats work the same way for a pitcher. For example, Rockies starter Ubaldo Jimenez went into an interleague game against the Red Sox on June 23, 2010, with a sizzling ERA of 1.15. Up to that game, he had given up 13 earned runs over 101.1 innings.

$$(13 / 101.333) * 9 = 1.1546$$

However, the Red Sox slammed him that game for six earned runs in 5.2 innings. With a total of 107 IP and 19 ER, his ERA jumped to 1.60.

$$(19 / 107) * 9 = 1.5981$$

UBALDO JIMENEZ

Later in the season, after having pitched lots of innings, it gets harder for a pitcher to lower his ERA. On August 10 Jimenez's ERA was 2.61—43 ER in 148.1 IP. In his start that day, he pitched seven innings and allowed only one ER. It lowered his ERA, but only to 2.55. To get an accurate projection of how a player is doing, you need more data than just a few games' worth.

LEAGUE AVERAGE

RYAN BRAUN

Looking at a batter's AVG and a pitcher's ERA is useful, but it becomes even more helpful in gauging his performance when you compare those stats to league averages. In 1968 Carl Yastrzemski's AVG was .301—good enough for first place in the majors. In 2010 Ryan Braun of the Milwaukee Brewers batted .304, but that was 18th in the majors. In 1968 the major league AVG was .237. The major league AVG in 2010 was .257. So Yastrzemski's average was 64 points above the league average in 1968, while Braun's was 57 points above the league average in 2010. So although Yastrzemski was first in the league for batting average while Braun was only 18th, the players performed about the same compared to the league average.

ADVANCED STATS

Baseball is definitely a game of stats. Besides basic stats such as batting average and ERA, there are many more stats used to get a more accurate measure of a player's value. For example, a hitting stat called Equivalent Average (EqA) compares batters' performances from different eras. This all-in-one stat includes base stealing and puts more emphasis on getting on base and hitting for power. EqA is a very complicated formula.

$$EqA = \frac{H + TB + 1.5\,(BB + HBP) + SB}{AB + BB + HBP + CS + SB/3}$$

EqA is on the same scale as AVG. So an EqA of .260 is average, .300 is good, and above .350 is really good.

That's a lot of numbers to work through, but the important thing to remember is that it is used for comparing players in different eras. For an example, Carl Yastrzemski's 1968 AVG of .301 equates to an EqA of .340. Because it was more difficult for players to get hits in 1968, Yastrzemski's EqA more accurately reflects what a great season he had as a hitter.

OPS is another stat used to more accurately represent a player's true offensive value. OPS is the sum of on base percentage and slugging percentage. It helps to compare batters if you want to account for their power—extra base hits—and ability to draw walks, two things not covered by batting average alone.

Babe Ruth, one of the best sluggers in the game, had an amazing 1.379 OPS in 1920.

.532 OBP + .847 SLG = 1.379 OPS

JOSH HAMILTON

PERCENT INCREASE

In 2009 Josh Hamilton of the Texas Rangers batted .268. But in 2010 he had an average of .359, which led the majors. To determine his percent increase, find the difference between the two numbers (.359 - .268 = .09). Then take the difference and divide it by the original number: .09 / .268 = .3358. To make this a percentage, multiply the number by 100 (.3358 * 100 = 33.58%). That's a spectacular improvement!

MATH OF THE GAME

You may know more baseball math than you think. When you throw the runner out at first base from the shortstop position, how does your arm know how high and how far to throw the ball? Did you do a quick math calculation to know what speed to put on the ball to be able to get it there before the runner? Not quite, but you did a quick estimate, and you might not have needed numbers to do it.

You probably did not really calculate that you were 120 feet from the first baseman's glove, so you would have to throw the ball 75 miles per hour to get it to him in .5 seconds. On the field you have to react too quickly to ponder all of those numbers. But it's fun to see how it all works!

Now you can use math to try to determine who was the best baseball player ever. Was it Ty Cobb because of his all-time high career AVG of .366? What about Ted Williams, whose career OBP was .482? Babe Ruth's career SLG was .690, better than anyone else in history. Maybe numbers can't settle any arguments about who was the best ever. But that's what makes sports—and math—fun!

FANTASY BASEBALL

Fantasy baseball allows fans to imagine they are big league managers. Each person in the fantasy league assembles a team from Major League players, but each baseball player can only be on one team. Then the teams are compared using the stats of the ballplayers against other teams in the fantasy league. The teams compare many stats, including HR, K, SB, and ERA. Points are scored differently, depending on the league. The teams with the most points make the playoffs, where they go head-to-head for the league championship. It's a great way for fans to track the stats of their favorite players!

GLOSSARY

area—the amount of surface within a specific boundary; area is measured in square units

batting average—a hitting statistic that measures how often a player gets a hit

diameter—the length of a straight line through the center of a circle

earned run average (ERA)—a pitching statistic used to measure how many earned runs a pitcher allows every nine innings

equivalent average (EqA)—a hitting statistic used to compare players from different eras

hypotenuse—the longest side of a right triangle

on base percentage (OBP)—a hitting statistic that measures how often a player gets on base

perimeter—the outside edge around a specific area

Pythagorean theorem—an equation used to find the third side of a right triangle ($a^2 + b^2 = c^2$)

radius—the length of a line drawn from the middle of a circle to the edge

ratio—a comparison of two quantities expressed in numbers

slugging percentage—a hitting statistic that measures the amount of total bases a player earns on hits compared to the number of at bats

WHIP—a pitching statistic that measures the number of walks and hits a pitcher allows per inning

READ MORE

Bertoletti, John C. *How Baseball Managers Use Math.* Math in the Real World. New York: Chelsea Clubhouse, 2010.

Buckley, James, Jr. *Ultimate Guide to Baseball.* Scholastic Ultimate Guides. New York: Shoreline Pub., 2010.

Minden, Cecilia, and Katie Marsico. *Baseball.* Real World Math, Sports. Ann Arbor, Mich.: Cherry Lake Pub., 2009.

INTERNET SITES

FactHound offers a safe, fun way to find Internet sites related to this book. All of the sites on FactHound have been researched by our staff.

Here's all you do:

Visit *www.facthound.com*

Type in this code: 9781429665698

 Check out projects, games and lots more at
www.capstonekids.com

INDEX